CONTENTS

INTRODUCTION

Focused. Talented. Hardworking. These are just a few of the words that describe star Major League Baseball player Bryce Harper. Harper has been ahead of the game since he was three years old. That is when he first began playing T-ball against much older kids. Many people who saw him play baseball when he was a child thought he would someday be on a professional team. Harper could hit better than everyone else. He could run fast. He could play several positions well. Harper could even pitch if his team needed him to do that.

Harper is naturally talented. But he has always worked hard to be the best possible baseball player he can be. He spends hours practicing his swing in the batting cage. He studies other players so he can learn from them. Harper is also a fierce competitor. He told the *Washington Post*, "I play the game hard, real hard. I respect everyone on the field. But if you're on the other team, I'm trying to beat you."

As a sophomore in high school, Harper was so good that he caught the eye of *Sports Illustrated*. He was put on the cover of the magazine when he was just sixteen years old. When asked about his goals, he said, to "be in the [Baseball] Hall of Fame, definitely. … Be considered the greatest baseball player who ever lived."

After his sophomore year of high school, Harper took a test that allowed him to graduate early. He went on to junior college and joined the baseball team. After one successful year in junior college, the Washington Nationals drafted Harper. He was only seventeen years old.

Harper quickly moved up the ranks of the Nationals' minor league teams. After a little more than one season in the minor leagues, Harper joined the Nationals'

SPORTS' TOP MVPS™

BRYCE HARPER

SIMONE PAYMENT

rosen publishing's
rosen central®
New York

Published in 2019 by The Rosen Publishing Group, Inc.
29 East 21st Street, New York, NY 10010

First Edition

Library of Congress Cataloging-in-Publication Data

Names: Payment, Simone, author.
Title: Bryce Harper / Simone Payment.
Description: New York : Rosen Central, 2019. | Series: Sports' Top MVPs | Includes bibliographical references and index. | Audience: Grades: 5–8.
Identifiers: LCCN 2017047077| ISBN 9781508182047 (library bound) | ISBN 9781508182054 (paperback)
Subjects: LCSH: Harper, Bryce, 1992– —Juvenile literature. | Baseball players—United States—Biography—Juvenile literature.
Classification: LCC GV865.H268 P39 2019 | DDC 796.357092 [B]—dc23
LC record available at https://lccn.loc.gov/2017047077

Manufactured in the United States of America

On the cover: Bryce Harper bats against the Miami Marlins at Nationals Park on August 10, 2017, in Washington, DC.

Harper's coach in high school, Sam Thomas, says that if you spend any time at all around Harper, "you can't help but root for him."

major league team. Since then, he has been a superstar. He won the National League Rookie of the Year award. In 2015, he was named the National League Most Valuable Player. He makes the All-Star team year after year.

Bryce Harper has won awards and been praised all his life. His teammates respect him. His coaches have always loved him. Even players on other teams praise him. But he does not pay too much attention to all of that. Harper focuses on himself. He believes he can get even better. He told *Sports Illustrated*, "I'm not done yet. I still have work to do."

CHAPTER ONE

ALWAYS A STEP AHEAD

For someone who has always been one step ahead of everyone else, Bryce started life just a little bit behind. When Bryce Aron Max Harper was born on October 16, 1992, he seemed to be a fine, healthy baby. But a few minutes later, he started turning gray. The doctors discovered he had a hole in his heart. He also had pneumonia and had to be in an incubator. Bryce had to stay in the hospital for about three months.

When Bryce was well enough, he went home with his family. The Harper family lived in Las Vegas, where both of Bryce's parents had grown up. His mother, Sheri, was a paralegal. His father, Ron, was a steelworker. Sheri and Ron had met and started dating in seventh grade. Bryce has an older sister named Brittany and an older brother named Bryan.

The Harpers are a close family and enjoy doing things together. Growing up, Ron had played baseball and football and loved playing sports with Bryan and Bryce. Bryce looked up to his brother and always wanted to do whatever Bryan was doing.

IT ALL STARTED WITH T-BALL

When Bryce was just three years old, he joined a T-ball team with Bryan. Like Bryan, all the other kids on the team were six years old. Even

When Harper was fifteen, Damon Oppenheimer, a scout for the Yankees, saw him at the Area Code Games. Oppenheimer noticed how hard Harper worked and called the young player "the real deal."

though everyone else was older, Bryce was already so good at baseball that he fit right in. At a T-ball game when Bryce was four or five years old, Bryce's uncle called him Mondo. That nickname stuck. Close friends and family still call him Mondo.

From an early age, Bryce was obsessed with baseball. He loved to watch games and study famous players. He loved the New York Yankees, and his favorite player was Mickey Mantle. Mantle had been a star Yankees' player in the 1950s and 1960s. Even though Mantle had played long before Bryce was born, Bryce knew all about him. He had a poster of Mantle on his bedroom wall. His grandfather had gotten it for him. He also wore the number 7 on his baseball uniforms when he was young. That is the number Mantle had worn. When Bryce joined a new team when he was ten years old, someone already on the team wore the number 7. Bryce decided to wear 34, because 3 + 4 = 7.

ON THE ROAD

Bryce played on T-ball and then baseball teams, always with older kids. These were local teams, made up of kids who lived nearby. It was clear from early on that Bryce was a very talented baseball player. So when he was nine years old, he joined a team that traveled to tournaments around the country. This team was made up of the best players from the Las Vegas area. They played other teams made up of top players from other cities. Sometimes, Bryce's mother or father would travel with him to these weekend tournaments. Sometimes, he went on his own. Each year, he would play 80 to 130 games, all around the United States. Bryce loved meeting and playing against top players and traveling to new places.

Bryce loved baseball so much that after a long weekend of travel and playing in tournaments he would return home and still want to go to the batting cage to practice his swing. He would be so eager to play that he would be ready for his game many hours before it started. One day, when he was about nine years old, Bryce's father got up to go to work at 4 a.m. He saw Bryce in his room, already dressed in his baseball uniform.

It was clear that Bryce was an extremely talented baseball player. His mother realized just how special he was after a game when he was about twelve years old. He was playing in a tournament in Alabama. During the tournament, he batted twelve times. Out of those twelve at-bats, he hit eleven home runs. The only time he didn't hit a home run, he hit a double.

Bryce's father spent hours helping him improve his baseball skills. Ron worked at his steelworker job from 4 a.m. until noon. After school, Ron would pitch baseballs to Bryce and Bryan. He would write numbers on the ball and pitch them to the boys. Bryce and Bryan

Harper says that his dad (pictured here with Bryce at the 2013 Home Run Derby) "worked so hard to make life good for my whole family."

would have to call out the numbers they saw on the baseballs speeding toward them. Ron would also pitch them tiny objects like bottle caps or sunflower seeds. They were hard to see and would not move in a predictable way, as a baseball would. This way, the boys would focus on the object and improve their eye-hand coordination. Ron would also bring home heavy steel bars from work. Bryce would swing these twenty-five-pound (eleven-kilogram) pieces of steel instead of a bat. Bryce loved this time he spent with his dad. He also appreciated what his dad taught him about the importance of hard work.

When Bryce wasn't focused on baseball, he was just a regular kid. He played football and snowboarded. He loved playing with Harley, the family's yellow Labrador retriever. Bryce volunteered regularly, and got good

As a catcher on his high school team, Harper looked up to professional catchers Johnny Bench, Joe Mauer, and Iván "Pudge" Rodríguez.

grades in school. He also went to church with his family. The Harper family is Mormon and went to church most Sundays.

LOOKING AHEAD

By the time Bryce got to high school, he was already thinking ahead to playing professional baseball. He had many different skills. He was an amazing hitter. He was also extremely fast when running the bases. Most of the time, Bryce played catcher on his high school team. But, he told the *Washington Post*, "I'll play anywhere they put me. I'll play outfield. I'll play third.... I'll do what anybody needs." Sometimes Bryce even pitched. In fact, he could throw a baseball 96 miles per hour (154 kilometer per hour).

Bryan was a senior in high school when Bryce was a freshman, and they played on the high school team together. Bryan knew Bryce was going to be a baseball superstar the day Bryce hit a 570-foot (174-meter) grand slam. In that same game, Bryce hit another homer that slammed into the scoreboard.

While he was in high school, Bryce continued to play in tournaments on a travel team. He also played for the United States in the Pan Am Championship in Mexico when he was fifteen. The US team played eight games, and during those games, Bryce hit four home runs, his batting average was .571, and he stole six bases. He even pitched the eleventh inning of one of the games and was named most valuable player (MVP).

Bryce also played in the Area Code Games in Long Beach, California, that year. The other players on the teams were seventeen and eighteen years old, but even against those older players Bryce stood out. Scouts for Major League Baseball (MLB) teams noticed how hard he hit the ball. They also noticed how hard he worked and how seriously he took the game.

SPORTS ILLUSTRATED COVER BOY

Major League Baseball scouts weren't the only ones who noticed how talented Bryce was. Anyone interested in sports, baseball in particular, became aware of Bryce on June 8, 2009. That day, Bryce was featured on the cover of *Sports Illustrated* magazine. He was only sixteen years old but was now a household name. *Sports Illustrated* compared him to LeBron James, the basketball superstar who had been a top high school player and to golfer Tiger Woods. They also compared him to Alex Rodriguez, who had been a very talented baseball player at a young age. But they thought Bryce was even better than Rodriguez. *Sports Illustrated* correctly predicted that Bryce would become a baseball superstar.

THE PLAN

By the time Bryce finished his sophomore year of high school at age sixteen, he was 6 feet 3 inches (1.9 m) tall and 205 pounds (93 kg). He had been on the cover of *Sports Illustrated*. It was clear he could compete against older, better players. He was so good he could probably already play for an MLB team. Bryce's parents and his coaches knew that baseball was all Bryce wanted to do. They all knew that playing high school baseball wasn't enough for Bryce. They decided he could take the general educational development (GED) test. If he passed, that would be the same as graduating from high school. Then he could go to junior college. It would be the next step on the path to playing baseball in the major leagues.

CHAPTER TWO

ON THE PATH TO THE MAJOR LEAGUES

At the end of his sophomore year of high school, Bryce took the GED exam and passed. In August, instead of starting his junior year of high school, he would be headed to junior college at the College of Southern Nevada. There he would play for its baseball team, the Coyotes.

JUNIOR COLLEGE

Bryce had always competed against kids who were several years older than he was. This would also be true at junior college, but he was ready for the challenge. He was eager to face better competition and continue to prepare for the major leagues.

There were two things that helped Bryce make the transition to junior college. First Bryan transferred from the college he had been attending in California to join Bryce at the College of Southern Nevada. Bryan would be pitching for the baseball team. And Bryce continued to live at home so he would have the support of his family.

Bryce tried to live the normal life of a teenager who would be in high school, even though he was at college. His girlfriend was still in high school so he got time off from school and practice to do things like attend the homecoming dance. Bryce also tried to attend church each Sunday with his family.

At the end of the regular season, Harper had more home runs, runs batted in, and runs than anyone else in the Scenic West Athletic Conference.

However, Bryce's life was far from normal. After the *Sports Illustrated* cover story, there were many who wanted to interview him, including *60 Minutes*, Jimmy Kimmel, and CNN. Bryce turned down all the interview requests. But all the attention did add to the pressure he felt to prove he was as good a baseball player as everyone was saying he was.

Bryce also wanted to do well in college. During his first semester, he did very well in school. The pressure was getting to him, though, and he began to lose weight. And he was not hitting well at baseball practice. His coach noticed this. In October, he asked Bryce to take eight days off from practice and just rest. This made Bryce question if he had made the right decision in going to junior college. He was eager to get back to hitting and practicing.

OUTSIDE SUPPORT

When Bryce was just ten years old, Scott Boras, one of the top agents for baseball players, went to a baseball tournament where one of his sons was playing. Boras saw Bryce playing in this tournament and was extremely impressed. Boras was good at judging talent. He could not be Bryce's agent until he was ready to become a professional baseball player. However, Boras sent Kurt Stilwell, a former MLB player for the Cincinnati Reds and San Diego Padres, to advise Bryce. Stilwell helped Bryce and his family make decisions and prepare for a career in the major leagues.

READY FOR SOME COMPETITION

Throughout the fall, Bryce and his teammates on the Coyotes practiced for the spring baseball season. Bryce could not wait for them to play together as a team. He also wanted to prove that he was good enough to soon head to a major league team.

In his first game with the Coyotes, the stadium was crowded with people waiting to see him play. Bryce did not disappoint. Although he walked in the first inning, he hit a single and scored a run in the second. In the eighth inning, he hit a sacrifice fly and the Coyotes won 11–4.

The Coyotes had a very successful season, and the spring went by quickly for Bryce. With his focus on playing baseball, he did not do as well in his classes. Unlike in the first semester, when he had earned As and Bs, in the spring he got Bs and Cs and even a failing grade in his writing course. However, his baseball playing was as terrific as everyone had expected it to be. Over the season, he hit thirty-one

On a day he played a double header with the Coyotes, Harper got no hits. After those two games, he practiced in the batting cage, watched videos, and the next day hit a home run.

home runs. That was more than anyone else playing college baseball that year. Bryce's batting average for the season was an impressive .431.

During the season, people sometimes criticized him for being immature. They seemed to forget that he was just seventeen years old. But most people, including coaches for opposing teams, respected him. They saw how hard he played, how much he practiced, and how much he focused on being the best player he could be.

At the end of the regular season, the Coyotes went to the Junior College World Series. They made it to the final round, and the Coyotes seemed to be on track to win. However, in the second-to-last game, Bryce argued with the umpire after being called out on a play. He was ejected from the game and would not be allowed to play the next game either. In that next game, the Coyotes lost and the season was over. Bryce told Rob Miech, who wrote a book about him, "It was not the storybook ending I thought it would be. We tried our hardest. … [W]e got pretty far, but it didn't happen."

APPEARANCES COUNT

When Bryce was about seven years old, he saw college football players wearing eye-black stripes, stripes painted under the eyes to reduce glare. Bryce thought they looked very cool and decided to start wearing them himself. Some people made fun of him for this, but he continued anyway. Putting them on became part of his routine, and it helped him prepare for a game.

Now when he looks at himself in the mirror and sees the stripes, it helps him focus on the game ahead. Bryce is also known for his long, stylish hair. His sister is a hair stylist, and he often lets her try out new styles and even colors on his hair.

Even though the Coyotes didn't win the Junior College World Series, Bryce racked up some impressive awards. He won the Player of the Year for the Scenic West Athletic Conference. He also won the Golden Spikes Award for the best amateur baseball player.

After the season, Bryce was looking forward to having some time off. He wanted to hang out with his friends, go fishing, and spend time with his dog. However, there were a few other things that were going to be happening that summer. Bryce's life was about to change again in a major way.

CHAPTER THREE

DRAFTED!

While Harper was playing college baseball, many people were keeping an eye on his progress. One person who went to several of Harper's games was Mike Rizzo, the general manager of the Washington Nationals. The Nationals would have the first pick in the 2010 Major League Baseball draft. Rizzo was very impressed not only with Harper's playing skills but also by how mature Harper was and how hard he played. Rizzo knew there was a lot of pressure on Harper, but Harper seemed to be handling it well. Rizzo thought his ability to handle pressure along with his incredible baseball talent would help him do well in the major leagues.

THE BIG DAY

June 7, 2010, was draft day. Harper tried not to think about it too much. He wanted to enjoy his summer and have fun with his family and friends. Harper considered whether he should spend another year playing baseball in junior college. He discussed his plans with his family, but they knew that all he wanted to do was play professional baseball. Harper's father talked to Rob Miech for his book *Phenom: The Making of Bryce Harper*. He told Miech that when he asked Bryce what he wanted to do, Bryce told him, "I want to play pro ball. … It's what I want to do in my heart. I've always wanted to do it. It's my dream."

Harper was not nervous waiting for the draft. Playing professional baseball had always been his goal, and he worked as hard as he could to reach that goal.

After deciding to play professional baseball, Harper hired Scott Boras to be his agent. On the day of the draft, Harper was in Boras's office in Newport Beach, California. They waited to see if the Washington Nationals would pick him first. They did. This was the first time a junior college baseball player was chosen first in the draft. The Nationals decided Harper would play right field. Harper was excited to be headed to the major leagues. The deal was not official yet, though. He would have to wait just a little longer.

WAITING TO PLAY

With the draft over, it was a waiting game. First, Harper had to wait until his deal was finalized with the Nationals. Then he had to wait until

THE WASHINGTON NATIONALS AND THE FIRST PICK

Since 1891, several professional baseball teams have played in Washington, DC. Those teams all eventually moved to other cities. One former Washington team became the Minnesota Twins. Another became the Texas Rangers. The team that now plays in Washington was originally the Montreal Expos. In 2005, the Expos moved to Washington and became the Nationals.

The years between 2005 and when Harper signed in 2010 were not good ones for the team. The Nationals had a losing record every year. But this actually helped them try to rebuild. Each year, Major League Baseball holds a draft. Teams choose the players they would like to join their team. The team with the worst record from the previous year is allowed to pick first. In 2009, the Washington Nationals had won just 59 games and lost 103. With that record, they were given the chance to make the first pick of available players in 2010.

spring training started. It would be a long wait for spring training: about eight months. Harper took advantage of this time off that summer. Right after the draft, he went to a Los Angeles Angels of Anaheim game versus the Texas Rangers. He went as a guest of Boras. He also attended the MLB All-Star Game in Anaheim, California. Harper then went fishing in Oklahoma with a friend. He did other fun things with friends from high school and with his family.

As Harper waited for his deal with the Nationals to be finalized, he started to get impatient. He even considered going back to junior college instead. However, right at the signing deadline in August, he made his deal with the Nationals official. They would pay him $9.9 million for a five-year deal. There were some extra things in the deal that could pay him $1 million more.

At the press conference announcing his signing, star Nationals first baseman Ryan Zimmerman helped Harper put on his jersey.

On August 26, 2010, the Nationals officially announced the signing of Harper at a press conference. Before the conference, Harper had a chance to take batting practice with the Nationals' players who would soon be his teammates. At the press conference, he got his jersey with the number 34 on it. He told the press that taking batting practice in Nationals Park had "felt like home" and that he was so happy to be there that he was "like a kid in a candy store."

MORE STEPS IN THE JOURNEY

Now that Harper was officially a National, it was time to start playing baseball. In September, Harper played in the Nationals' instructional league in Viera, Florida. In October, soon after his eighteenth birthday, Harper joined the Arizona Fall League. He played for the Scottsdale Scorpions. In the fall league, he played two games a week but practiced every day. Like so many other teams he had played on, Harper was the youngest player on the team. He learned a lot from his teammates and made many adjustments that improved his hitting and fielding.

While Harper was playing in the instructional leagues, his high school classmates were starting their senior year. It was strange for Harper to think of them in school while he was preparing to play in the major leagues.

Harper was also getting used to having millions of dollars. He used some of the money he got from signing to help pay for his sister's wedding. He also gave his brother money for college. For himself, he splurged on a Mercedes-Benz.

After the Arizona Fall League was over, Harper lived at home and went to early-morning workouts. In the afternoons, he would go to see his high school friends play in baseball games. He would also practice in the batting cage. In January, he went to the MLB media orientation. There he learned how to answer questions from reporters and how to deal with the public.

SPRING TRAINING

In February, it was finally time for spring training. Harper couldn't wait to get started. He wanted to show everyone that he was worth his giant contract. He wanted to live up to the hype. Harper told the *Washington Post*, "I want to be the best. I want to be perfect in every aspect of the game." Harper's family did not worry too much about Harper leaving home for the first time to start his MLB career. They knew he had a good foundation and they trusted him. They knew he would work hard and keep his focus on baseball.

Harper's first official workout with the Nationals was in the Instructional League in September 2010, where he began learning all about playing in the major leagues.

Harper headed to spring training in Port St. Lucie, Florida. He did not drive the Mercedes he had bought after being signed. Instead, he took his truck that already had 130,000 miles on it. He told the *Washington Post*, "That's my work truck. I want everyone to know I'm there for work."

Spring training began February 28, and Harper did work hard. He learned from his new teammates and started to prove he would be a star. During spring training, his batting average was .389. At the end of March, it was time for the Nationals' 2011 season to begin.

CHAPTER FOUR

THE BIG TIME

Harper began the 2011 MLB season playing for the Hagerstown Suns in Maryland. The Suns were the single-A class minor league team of the Nationals. Harper did so well in single-A that he was quickly promoted to the Nationals' double-A team in Harrisburg, Pennsylvania. Harper spent the rest of the season playing for the Harrisburg Senators.

Harper gets ready to bat in a May 2011 game for the Hagerstown Suns. By July 4, he had moved up to double-A Harrisburg.

THE MAJOR LEAGUES

Some baseball players spend several years working their way up through the minor leagues before they join a major league team. Not Harper. After just one year playing for the single-A and double-A Nationals' teams, Harper was almost there. The Nationals thought he was close to being able to join the major league team. But he needed to work some more on his fielding. They also wanted to give him time to ease into the 2012 season.

DAVEY JOHNSON

In Harper's first season with the Nationals, he was just nineteen years old. His manager was Davey Johnson, who was sixty-nine. Johnson was the oldest manager in the MLB at that time. Even though there was a fifty-year age difference between them, Harper and Johnson had very similar goals and values. They both believed in the importance of hard work. And they both were hoping for a winning season for the Nationals. Johnson had been a top MLB player for the Baltimore Orioles and Atlanta Braves. He had won two World Series rings with the Orioles. He had also managed four other MLB teams before the Nationals. As manager, he had won a World Series with the New York Mets.

Harper started the season on the triple-A team in Syracuse, New York. But he was not there long. After just twenty-one games in Syracuse, he was called up to join the Nationals. On April 28, 2012, Harper played in his first major league game, against the Los Angeles Dodgers. His first major league hit was a double.

A few days later, Harper had an unusual first stolen base. In a game against the Phillies, Harper was hit by a pitch from Cole Hamels and sent to first base. He moved up to third base on a hit from Jayson Werth. While at third base, Harper carefully watched the pitcher. Hamels threw to first base once, to keep Werth from stealing. The second time Hamels threw to first, Harper took a chance. He dashed to home and was safe. He had stolen a base and scored a run at the same time. Harper gave high-fives to some teammates and met his coach Davey Johnson on the top step of the dugout for another high-five.

Harper had several other firsts in May, such as his first major league home run on May 14. But Harper also made news with his behavior. During one game, he was frustrated and hit his bat against the wall. A splinter from the bat hit him above his eye, and he got a cut. He put a bandage on it, but the cut was deep and kept bleeding. He wanted to continue playing, but eventually he had to leave the game and got ten stitches.

There were lots of things to get used to about playing on a major league team. For one, he had to get used to being interviewed before and after games. Harper told the *Washington Post* that he actually liked talking to the media. "It's a blast. I love people knowing where I came from and what I'm about." But Harper did not like all questions that

Being interviewed before or after a game is part of the job of playing professional baseball. Here, Harper is interviewed before the 2016 All-Star Game.

reporters asked him. In June, the Nationals were playing in Toronto, Canada. In Canada, the legal drinking age is nineteen and a reporter asked if he had a favorite beer. Of course, in the United States where the drinking age is twenty-one, Harper could not legally drink. And as part of Harper's Mormon religion, drinking is not allowed. Harper replied to the reporter, "I'm not answering that. That's a clown question, bro." Harper's reply became a catchphrase, and soon there were T-shirts for sale with "That's a clown question, bro" printed on them.

In July, Harper played in his first MLB All-Star Game. Harper was chosen to go as a replacement for Marlins player Giancarlo Stanton, who was injured. Harper was very excited to be chosen and to be playing with the top players in the MLB. He was also the first position player to go to the All-Star Game as a teenager.

Over the 2012 season, Harper made amazing progress as a player. His teammates noticed and were glad to have him on their team. The Nationals' first baseman that year was Adam LaRoche. LaRoche had first seen Harper play in spring training of 2011. He told the *Augusta Chronicle* that Harper had "come a long way. … He's grown up a ton. He's got the respect of his teammates and we all back him 100 percent."

In the last full month of the 2012 season, Harper was one of the best players in the game. He had the most runs of any National League player, with twenty-seven, and was in the top five in many other statistics. Harper also won the National League Rookie of the Year award. He was the youngest player ever to win that award. He finished the year with twenty-two home runs, ninety-eight runs, and fifty-seven extra-base hits.

FIRST FULL SEASON IN THE MAJOR LEAGUES

Before the 2013 season, Harper was invited to play for the United States in the World Baseball Classic. He decided not to join the team because he wanted to focus on his upcoming season with the Nationals.

Even though he played many different positions when he was growing up, as a professional player he has only been an outfielder, usually playing right field.

When the 2013 season got under way, Harper had an amazing April. He hit nine home runs and was batting .334. In the middle of May, Harper was chasing down a ball in Dodger Stadium and ran into the scoreboard. He had to have eleven stitches in his chin. Worse, he injured his knee. He tried to keep playing but had to go on the disabled list (DL) on June 1 to rest his knee. It was hard for Harper to sit on the bench and not be on the field with his teammates. He missed about a month, returning on July 1. In his first time up to the plate when he returned, he hit a home run.

HARPER'S HEROES

In 2013, Harper teamed up with the Leukemia and Lymphoma Society to create Harper's Heroes. Harper's Heroes invites children who have cancer to come to Nationals games. They get to meet Harper and enjoy the game. Harper also raises money for the Leukemia and Lymphoma Society. He has raised money by designing special hats. Sales from the New Era hats help support cancer research.

Harper played in the All-Star Game soon after coming off the DL. He also participated in the Home Run Derby. He came in second, hitting twenty-four homers.

Harper struggled a bit after the All-Star Game in 2013. He was not hitting well. Until July 25, that is. That day, the Nationals were playing the Pittsburgh Pirates and Harper hit the first walk-off home run of his MLB career. His season improved after that, and he ended the season with twenty home runs and stats similar to those of his 2012 season.

CHAPTER FIVE

RISING TO THE TOP

Harper had played well in his first few seasons in the major leagues. But he was hoping for more. He wanted to be the best he could be. And, like most MLB players, he wanted to win a World Series.

However, Harper's knee injury in May 2013 had really affected his season. He missed a month and was not in top form once he returned to the field. So, before the 2014 season, Harper had surgery on his injured knee. The surgery seemed to help, and Harper had a good April. He was hitting well and playing well.

But in late April, Harper was injured again when he slid into third base. At first he thought he had sprained his thumb. However, it was more serious than that and he had to have surgery and go on the DL again. Harper missed fifty-seven games. He had a hard time getting into the groove when he returned from the DL. But, in the last month and a half of the season, Harper began hitting well again.

Even better than the fact that he was healthy and hitting well again, the Nationals finally made the playoffs. They would face the San Francisco Giants in the Division Series. Harper was excited to finally have a chance to win a World Series trophy. During the series, Harper hit three home runs in four games. However, the Nationals lost to the Giants, three games to one.

Harper tied up the fourth game of the NLDS with the Giants with a solo home run. Harper's homer was not enough, though, and the Nationals ended up losing the game.

TOP OF THE CHARTS

Harper was disappointed that his team did not make it to the next round in the playoffs. He also had another disappointment when he and his long-time girlfriend called off their wedding. But he looked ahead to the 2015 season hoping to do better. Before and during the season, he worked hard on his swing. He spent hours in the batting cage.

In 2015, he did play better. Harper was healthy all season long. In May, he hit three home runs in one game. In July, he played in his third All-Star Game. By the end of the season, he had hit an impressive forty-two home

A BIG ENDORSEMENT

Companies often pay athletes to represent their products. In 2011, Harper had signed a deal to endorse Under Armour athletic wear. In 2016, Under Armour signed him to a new deal for another ten years.

It was reported to be the largest deal ever for an MLB player. Harper also represents New Era hats, Gatorade, nutrition company MusclePharm, and Warriorblack eye black.

runs and scored 118 runs. His batting average was .330. He won the Silver Slugger Award and the National League Hank Aaron Award. Even better, he was voted the National League Most Valuable Player. Harper told MLB.com, "I'm very excited and very humbled to get this award." Harper had had only one goal for the season: "All I wanted to do was stay healthy, be on the field every single day."

Harper impressed everyone with his dedication, hard work, and amazing statistics. However, as a team the Nationals did not do as well in 2015 as they had the previous season. They did not make the playoffs. Harper would have to wait another year for a try at the World Series.

TRYING AGAIN

During the winter, Harper looked ahead to the coming season. He told *Rolling Stone* magazine, "I can't wait to get out there. I don't set goals, I just go out there and play." By the first day of January, he had started practicing his swing and preparing for the season.

Harper has played in nearly every All-Star Game since 2012. At the 2016 game, he had his first All-Star Game hit, a double.

In 2016, Harper had another season without any major injuries. But he did not hit quite as well as he had in 2015. Still, he went to the All-Star Game again, for the fourth time. In April, he hit his one hundredth home run. And, although Harper was not at the top of his game, as he was in 2015, the Nationals finished the 2016 regular season with ninety-five wins and a spot in the playoffs.

In the first round of the playoffs, the Nationals faced the Los Angeles Dodgers. Although Harper got four hits and stole three bases during the playoffs, the Nationals lost to the Dodgers in five games. They would have to wait another year.

While Harper waited for another season to start, he married Kayla Varner in San Diego, California, in December. After calling off their wedding in early 2015, this time they were ready. Harper and Kayla had met in high school. Kayla is an athlete as well. She played soccer in high school and college.

A NEW YEAR

The 2017 season got off to a good start for Harper. On May 17, he hit a home run in Pittsburgh, in a game against the Pirates. A home run wasn't normally a big deal for Harper. This one was special because he had now hit a home run in every National League ballpark.

Once again, in July, Harper headed to the All-Star Game as a starter. He got a hit and made an excellent diving catch. Harper's season continued on track after the All-Star break. By August 12, he had already hit more home runs than he had in his whole 2016 season. He had a .326 batting average and had driven in eighty-seven runs. But on August 12, he slipped on first base, which was wet. He got a bone bruise on his knee and had to go on the DL. Harper missed forty-two games and finally returned on September 26. The Nationals had missed Harper's excellent hitting. But the Nationals were once again headed to the playoffs.

Number 34 often comes through, as Harper did in this game on June 23, 2017, versus the Cincinnati Reds. He hit a game-winning single in the tenth inning.

The Nationals faced the Chicago Cubs in the first round of the playoffs. Harper was the hero in Game 2 of the playoffs, hitting a home run that tied the game. But once again, Harper and the Nationals did not make it past the first round. They lost to the Cubs in Game 5. After the game Harper told reporters he and his teammates put their "heart and soul into [the] game," but that they "just came up short." Harper would have to work hard, as he always does, and try again the next season.

FACT SHEET

Full name
Bryce Aron Max Harper
Birth date
October 16, 1992
Hometown
Las Vegas, Nevada
Height
6 feet 3 inches (1.91 m)
Weight
230 pounds (100 kg)
High school
Las Vegas High School
Junior college
College of Southern Nevada
Team
Washington Nationals
Bats
Left
Throws
Right

Past positions
Catcher, left field, pitcher
Current position
Right field
Uniform number
34
Amateur awards
Golden Spikes (2010), Player of the Year for Scenic West Athletic Conference (2010)
MLB awards
National League Rookie of the Year (2012), NL Hank Aaron Award (2015), NL Most Valuable Player (2015)
All-Star teams
2012, 2013, 2015, 2016, 2017

TIMELINE

1992 Bryce Aron Max Harper is born on October 16, in Las Vegas, Nevada.

2009 Harper is featured on the cover of the *Sports Illustrated* June 8 issue. He gets his GED and enters the College of Southern Nevada.

2010 Harper wins the Golden Spikes Award as the best amateur baseball player in America. He is drafted by the Washington Nationals on June 7. The Nationals announce his official signing on August 26. Harper plays in the Arizona Fall League.

2011 Harper attends his first spring training. He plays on the Nationals' single-A and double-A teams.

2012 Harper starts the MLB season on the Nationals' triple-A team. He is called up to the major league team on April 28. He plays in his first All-Star Game and wins the National League Rookie of the Year.

2013 Harper plays his first full season with the Nationals. He plays in the All-Star Game and participates in the Home Run Derby.

2014 Harper has off-season knee surgery. The Nationals go to the playoffs but lose in the first round to the San Francisco Giants.

2015 Harper plays in the All-Star Game. He wins the Silver Slugger Award, the Hank Aaron Award, and the National League Most Valuable Player.

2016 Harper plays in the All-Star Game. The Nationals go to the playoffs but lose in the first round to the Los Angeles Dodgers. He marries Kayla Varner in December.

2017 Harper plays in the All-Star Game. The Nationals go to the playoffs but lose in the first round to the Chicago Cubs.

GLOSSARY

amateur A person who takes part in something without getting paid.

catchphrase A word or phrase that becomes well known and repeated.

contract A legal agreement between two parties.

draft The process of choosing players to join a team.

endorsement Official approval or support of something.

eye black A black grease or plastic strip put under the eyes to reduce glare from the sun or lights.

eye-hand coordination A person's sight and hands working together to perform a certain movement.

foundation Strong support or background.

general educational development (GED) test A group of four tests that measure a person's knowledge of academic subjects.

general manager A person who hires the coaching staff for a baseball team and decides which players to add or trade from a team.

incubator A box that keeps a premature or sick baby warm and protected.

leukemia Cancer of the blood.

lymphoma Cancer of the lymph nodes.

mature Fully grown or developed.

paralegal A person who assists a lawyer.

pneumonia A disease of the lungs usually caused by infection.

press conference A meeting where reporters interview one or more people.

semester A period of about eighteen weeks that forms half of a school year.

steelworker A person who works with steel to build buildings.

tournament A contest or series of contests that lead to a championship game.

travel team A sports team that plays games outside of the local area.

FOR MORE INFORMATION

Baseball Canada
2212 Gladwin Crescent, Suite A7
Ottawa, ON K1B 5N1
(613) 748-5606
Website: https://www.baseball.ca
Facebook: @baseballcanada
Twitter: @baseballcanada
Instagram: @baseballcanada
YouTube: @baseballcanadamedia
Baseball Canada oversees all aspects of baseball in Canada.

Canadian Baseball Network
271 Brock Street
Peterborough, ON K9H 2P8
Website: https://www.canadianbaseballnetwork.com
Facebook: @canadianbaseballnetwork
Twitter: @CDNbaseball
Instagram: @cdnbaseball
The Canadian Baseball Network promotes Canadian baseball players and the Toronto Blue Jays.

Harper's Heroes
Leukemia and Lymphoma Society
3 International Drive, Suite 200
Rye Brook, NY 10573
(703) 399-2959
Website: https://www.lls.org/harpersheroes
The Leukemia and Lymphoma Society works to cure cancers of the blood. Harper's Heroes hosts kids who are battling a blood cancer at a Nationals game.

National Baseball Hall of Fame and Museum
25 Main Street
Cooperstown, NY 13326
(888) HALL-OF-FAME
Website: http://www.baseballhall.org
Facebook: @baseballhall
Twitter: @baseballhall
Instagram: @baseballhall
YouTube: @baseballhall
The Baseball Hall of Fame and Museum collects and displays everything having to do with the game of baseball and its players, managers, umpires, and team owners.

Washington Nationals
Nationals Park
1500 South Capitol Street SE
Washington, DC 20003
(202) 675-6287
Website: https://www.mlb.com/nationals
Facebook: @Nationals
Twitter: @Nationals
Instagram: @nationals
The Nationals are a Major League Baseball team in the National League. Their ballpark opened in 2008.

FOR FURTHER READING

Gitlin, Marty. *Bryce Harper: Baseball Superstar*. Burnsville, MN: Focus Readers, 2017.

Good, Ann Herndon. *Washington Nationals A–Z*. Herndon, VA: Mascot Books, 2017.

Graubart, Norman. *The Science of Baseball*. New York, NY: Rosen Publishing, 2016.

Hazelgrove, William. *The Pitcher*. Virginia Beach, VA: Kohler Books, 2013.

Kelley, K. C. *Baseball Superstars 2016*. New York, NY: Scholastic Inc., 2016.

Martirano, Ron. *Baseball: Great Records, Weird Happenings, Odd Facts, Amazing Moments & Other Cool Stuff*. Watertown, MA: Imagine Publishing, 2015.

Reavy, Kevin, and Ryan Spaeder. *Incredible Baseball Stats: The Coolest, Strangest Facts and Stats in Baseball History*. New York, NY: Sports Publishing, 2016.

Russell, Jake. *100 Things Nationals Fans Should Know and Do Before They Die*. Chicago, IL: Triumph Books, 2016.

Sonnenblink, Jordan. *Curveball: The Year I Lost My Grip*. New York, NY: Scholastic Books, 2014.

Sports Illustrated editors. *Baseball's Greatest*. New York, NY: Sports Illustrated, 2013.

Stanley, Glen, and Jason Porterfield. *An Insider's Guide to Baseball: Sports Tips, Techniques, and Strategies*. New York, NY: Rosen Publishing, 2015.

BIBLIOGRAPHY

Fendrich, Howard. "Age gap doesn't matter for Nationals' Bryce Harper, Davey Johnson." *Augusta Chronicle*, October 5, 2012. http://chronicle.augusta.com/sports-baseball/2012-10-05/age-gap-doesnt-matter-nationals-bryce-harper-davey-johnson.

Janes, Chelsea. "Bryce Harper unveils new limited edition hat line benefiting cancer charities." *Washington Post*, August 24, 2016. https://www.washingtonpost.com/news/nationals-journal/wp/2016/08/24/bryce-harper-unveils-limited-edition-hat-line-proceeds-to-benefit-leukemia-and-lymphoma-society/?utm_term=.c7b4eb148f23.

Kilgore, Adam. "Bryce Harper replaces Giancarlo Stanton, becomes the youngest position player in All-Star Game history." *Washington Post*, July 7, 2012. https://www.washingtonpost.com/blogs/nationals-journal/post/bryce-harper-replaces-giancarlo-stanton-becomes-the-youngest-position-player-in-all-star-game-history/2012/07/07/gJQAWKeoUW_blog.html?utm_term=.b05ac4667952.

Ladson, Bill. "Harper unanimous BBWWA NL MVP after huge year." MLB.com, November 19, 2015. http://m.mlb.com/news/article/157684172/nationals-bryce-harper-wins-nl-mvp-award.

Ladson, Bill. "Making His Mark." *Baseball Digest*, January/February 2016. pp. 20–23.

Landers, Chris. "Celebrate seven years of Bryce Harper with the best moment from each season." MLB.com Cut4. Retrieved August 18, 2017. http://m.mlb.com/cutfour/2017/08/16/248014822/best-moment-of-each-year-of-bryce-harpers-mlb-career.

Miech, Rob. *The Last Natural*. New York, NY: Thomas Dunne Press, St. Martin's Press, 2012.

Montgomery, James. "Bryce Harper on Killing His Hair and Keeping 'The Mighty Ducks' Alive." *Rolling Stone*, January 12, 2016. http://www.rollingstone.com/sports/features/bryce-harper-on-killing-his-hair-and-keeping-the-mighty-ducks-alive-20160112.

Sheinin, Dave. "Bryce Harper, potential No. 1 pick in the MLB draft, faces questions about his attitude, not his ability." *Washington Post*, May 16, 2010. http://www.washingtonpost.com/wp-dyn/content/article/2010/05/15/AR2010051503114.html.

Sheinin, Dave. "For the love of Bryce Harper: Get ready, Washington. You're about to fall head over heels for the Nationals' newest star." *Washington Post Magazine*, March 13, 2011. http://www.washingtonpost.com/wp-dyn/content/article/2011/03/10/AR2011031005325.html.

Verducci, Tom. "Baseball's LeBron." *Sports Illustrated*, June 8, 2009. https://www.si.com/vault/2009/06/08/105822135/baseballs-lebron.

Verducci, Tom. "The Man They Love to Hate." *Sports Illustrated*, March 30, 2015. pp. 82–86.

Verducci, Tom. "Season for the Ages." *Sports Illustrated*, October 5, 2015. pp. 36–39.

Worgo, Tom. "When Talent Matches Potential." *Baseball Digest*, September/October 2013. pp. 32–35.

INDEX

S

T

U

V

W

ABOUT THE AUTHOR

Simone Payment has a bachelor's degree in psychology from Cornell University and a master's degree in elementary education from Wheelock College. She is the author of numerous books for young adults. Her book about Navy SEALs, *Inside Special Operations: Navy SEALs* (also from Rosen Publishing), won a 2004 Quick Picks for Reluctant Young Readers award from the American Library Association and is on the Nonfiction Honor List of Voice of Youth Advocates. She is a lifelong baseball fan and avid follower of the Boston Red Sox.

PHOTO CREDITS

Cover, pp. 5, 23, 37 Greg Fiume/Getty Images; pp. 4–5 (background) Eugene Onischenko/Shutterstock.com; p. 8 Chris Trotman/Getty Images; pp. 10, 26, 33 The Washington Post/Getty Images; p. 11 Robert Beck /Sports Illustrated/Getty Images; pp. 15, 21 © AP Images; pp. 17, 25 Icon Sports Wire/Getty Images; pp. 28, 35 Harry How/Getty Images; p. 30 Dilip Vishwanat/Getty Images.

Design: Michael Moy; Photo Research: Karen Huang